Summer

by Terri DeGezelle

Consultant:
Joseph M. Moran, Ph.D.
Meteorologist
Education Program
American Meteorological Society

Bridgestone Books
an imprint of Capstone Press
Mankato, Minnesota

Bridgestone Books are published by Capstone Press
151 Good Counsel Drive, P.O. Box 669, Mankato, Minnesota 56002
http://www.capstone-press.com

Library of Congress Cataloging-in-Publication Data
DeGezelle, Terri, 1955–
     Summer / by Terri DeGezelle.
     p. cm.—(Seasons)
     Includes bibliographical references and index.
     Contents: Summer—Summer temperatures—Water in summer—Trees in summer—Animals in summer—People in summer—What causes summer?—Why do seasons change?—Seasons in other places—Hands on: earth's tilt in summer.
     ISBN 0-7368-1411-6 (hardcover)
     1. Summer—Juvenile literature. [1. Summer.] I. Title.
QB637.6 .D44 2003
508.2—dc21   2001008758

Summary: Explains why seasons change and describes the ways trees, animals, and people react to summer.

Editorial Credits
Christopher Harbo, editor; Karen Risch, product planning editor; Linda Clavel, designer and illustrator; Anne McMullen, illustrator; Alta Schaffer, photo researcher

Photo Credits
Corbis, cover (top left), 4, 8; Penny Tweedie, 21
James P. Rowan, 10, 12
Kent & Donna Dannen, 14
Photri-Microstock/Richard T. Nowitz, 6
RubberBall Productions, cover (bottom left)
Unicorn Stock Photos, cover (main photo); Mark E. Gibson, 20

Artistic Effects
Corbis; RubberBall Productions

Table of Contents

Fun Fact

The first day of summer is called the summer solstice.

4

Summer

Summer is the season between spring and autumn. June 21 or 22 is the first day of summer in the Northern Hemisphere. Summer lasts for three months. It is the hottest season of the year.

hemisphere
one half of Earth

Summer Temperatures

Outdoor temperatures can be hot in summer. Swimming pools and lakes become warm on hot days. People cool off with fans and air conditioners. Animals seek shelter from the Sun under shade trees.

air conditioner
a machine that cools indoor air

Fun Fact

The largest hailstone recorded was 17.5 inches (44 centimeters) around. It fell in Coffeyville, Kansas, on September 3, 1970.

Water in Summer

Thunderstorms form in summer. Heavy rains and hail can fall. Lightning can be dangerous. Crops need rain to grow in summer. A long period of time without rain is called a drought. Crops dry up and die during a drought.

Trees in Summer

Summer gives trees sunlight and rain to grow. Trees have green leaves during summer. Fruit trees are full of fruit. Apples, peaches, and pears ripen. During summer, trees grow new buds that will open in the following spring.

Animals in Summer

Young animals grow in summer. Birds bring worms to their young. Bees gather nectar from flowers. Butterflies fly among the flowers. Some animals' coats turn different colors. Snowshoe rabbits' white fur turns brown to blend in with the woods.

nectar
a sweet liquid that bees collect from flowers

People in Summer

People dress to stay cool in summer. They wear shorts and sandals. People swim to cool off. Families go fishing, biking, and camping. Boys and girls play baseball. Many schools close for summer vacation.

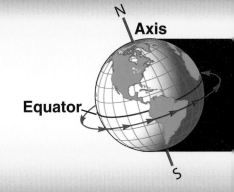

What Causes Summer?

Summer is caused by Earth's tilt. Earth spins like a top as it moves around the Sun. Earth spins on an axis. The axis is tilted. Summer begins when Earth's axis points toward the Sun. On the first day of summer, the Sun's rays center on places north of the equator.

axis
an imaginary line that runs through the middle of Earth from the North Pole to the South Pole

17

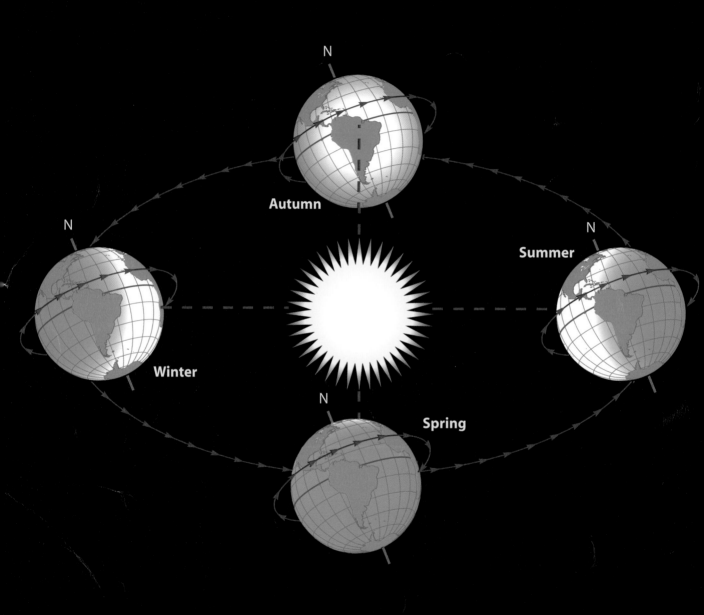

N

Autumn

N

Summer

N

Winter

N

Spring

Why Do Seasons Change?

Earth makes one trip around the Sun each year. Earth's movement and tilt cause seasons to change. The Northern Hemisphere leans toward the Sun in summer. The Sun is high in the sky. Daylight is longest in summer.

When the Northern Hemisphere has summer, the Southern Hemisphere has winter. Many children in the Northern Hemisphere enjoy summer vacation in June, July, and August.

At the same time of year, it is winter in the Southern Hemisphere. Most children are in school at this time.

Hands On: Earth's Tilt in Summer

Earth's tilt causes the seasons. Summer in the Northern Hemisphere happens when the North Pole is tilted toward the Sun. You can see how Earth's tilt creates summer.

What You Need

Globe
Table
Flashlight

What You Do

1. Place the globe on the table.
2. Tilt the globe slightly toward you.
3. Take five steps back from the globe.
4. Shine the flashlight at the globe so that the brightest spot shines on the Tropic of Cancer. The Tropic of Cancer is an imaginary line about halfway between the equator and the North Pole.
5. Summer begins in the Northern Hemisphere when the North Pole leans toward the Sun.

The light from the flashlight acts like the Sun's rays. Earth's tilt causes most of the sunlight to shine on the Northern Hemisphere. Look at the North Pole. It gets sunlight all day and all night during summer.

Words to Know

axis (AK-siss)—an imaginary line that runs through the middle of Earth from the North Pole to the South Pole

drought (DROUT)—a long period of time without rainfall

equator (i-KWAY-tur)—an imaginary line halfway between the North Pole and the South Pole

hemisphere (HEM-uhss-fihr)—one half of Earth; the Northern Hemisphere is north of the equator.

nectar (NEK-tur)—a sweet liquid that bees collect from flowers; bees turn nectar into honey.

season (SEE-zuhn)—one of four parts of the year; summer, autumn, winter, and spring are seasons.

tilt (TILT)—an angle to the left or right of center

Read More

Klingel, Cynthia Fitterer, and Robert B. Noyed. *Summer: A Level Two Reader.* Chanhassen, Minn.: Child's World, 2001.

Sipiera, Paul P., and Diane M. Sipiera. *The Seasons.* A True Book. New York: Children's Press, 1998.

Stille, Darlene R. *Summer.* Simply Science. Minneapolis: Compass Point Books, 2001.

Internet Sites

The Big Bang: All about Seasons
http://www.cbc4kids.ca/general/the-lab/big-bang/
00-03-23/default.html
Web Weather for Kids
http://www.ucar.edu/40th/webweather
What Causes the Seasons?
http://windows.arc.nasa.gov/tour/link=/
the_universe/uts/seasons1.html&edu=elem

Index